Junior Great Books®

Reader's Journal

Series 4   Book One

This book belongs to:

_____

The Great Books Foundation
A nonprofit educational organization

The interpretive discussion program that moves
students toward excellence in reading comprehension,
critical thinking, and writing

9 8 7 6 5 4 3 2
Printed in the United States of America

Cover art by Louise Brierley. Copyright 2006 by Louise Brierley.
Text and cover design by William Seabright, William Seabright & Associates.
Interior design by Think Design Group.

Published and distributed by

The Great Books Foundation
A nonprofit educational organization
35 East Wacker Drive, Suite 400
Chicago, IL 60601

Welcome *to Your Reader's Journal*

This Reader's Journal is a place for you to collect your thoughts about the Junior Great Books stories you read and discuss in class. Here, you can be an artist and a poet, while discovering some secrets to becoming a strong reader and writer.

There are many parts of the Reader's Journal:

Writing Notebook allows you to gather some of your favorite pieces of writing in one place to revise and polish them.

Curious Words is where you can record the strange or interesting words you come across while reading. You don't have to memorize these words—you get to play with them, sounding them out in your head or out loud or using them to make up messages and rhymes.

The **glossary** contains unusual or difficult words from the stories you've read. Look here for definitions that will help you better understand what you are reading.

Are you hunting for a **keeper question**, or do you have your **Head in the Clouds**? Maybe you're **Building Your Answer**, **Writing to Explain** or **Explore**, or getting **Into Reading**. Whatever you're working on, this Reader's Journal belongs to you. It's the place for your great ideas.

Contents

Thank You, M'am

by Langston Hughes

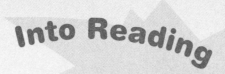

Into Reading

Asking Questions

Asking questions is an important part of understanding what you're reading. Read the following two passages from the story and write a question that you have about each one. Remember your questions as you read the story a second time.

Your questions might be about:

- Why a character does or says something

- Why something happens the way that it does

- What a word, phrase, or sentence means

- A place where you feel confused about what is happening

Passage 1 (page 12)

"Then, Roger, you go to the sink and wash your face," said the woman, whereupon she turned him loose—at last. Roger looked at the door—looked at the woman—looked at the door—*and went to the sink.*

Your question after reading this passage:

_____

_____

_____

_____

_____

Passage 2 (page 13)

But the boy took care to sit on the far side of the room, away from the purse, where he thought she could easily see him out of the corner of her eye if she wanted to. He did not trust the woman *not* to trust him. And he did not want to be mistrusted now.

Your question after reading this passage:

_____

_____

_____

_____

HEAD in the Clouds

Use your imagination! Choose one of the topics in the clouds and draw a picture or write a little more about the story.

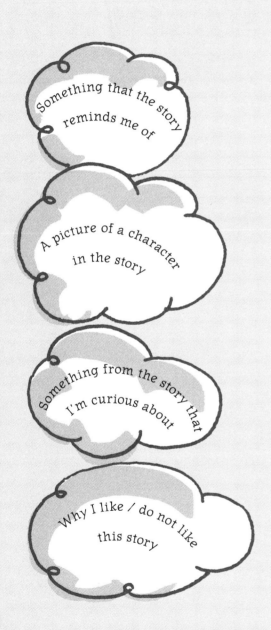

Something that the story reminds me of

A picture of a character in the story

Something from the story that I'm curious about

Why I like / do not like this story

Building Your Answer

The focus question:

_____

_____

_____

_____

Your answer before the discussion:

_____

_____

_____

_____

Your answer after the discussion (you may change or add to your first answer):

_____

_____

_____

_____

_____

Writing to Explain
A Clear Idea

Prewriting Notes

Write your answer after the discussion from the Building Your Answer page (page 5). Underline a part of your answer that you can write more about, and write your new answer with more details below.

Your new answer:

_____

_____

_____

_____

_____

_____

_____

_____

_____

_____

Writing to Explore
A Friendly Letter

Prewriting Notes

Complete this chart, choosing either Roger or Mrs. Jones to write a letter to the other character.

Salutation	Dear _____ ,
Details	1. _____
	_____
	_____
	_____
	2. _____
	_____
	_____
	_____
	3. _____
	_____
	_____
	_____
	_____
Closing (circle one)	Your friend, / Sincerely yours,
	_____

Writing to Explore
A Friendly Letter

Writing a Draft

Using your notes, write a draft of your letter in the space below.

A Letter from _____ **to** _____

Dear _____ ,

_____

_____

_____

_____

_____

_____

_____

_____

_____

_____

_____

Sincerely,

_____

The Gold Coin

by Alma Flor Ada

Keeper Question

In the space below, write a keeper question about the story that came into your mind during the first reading, while sharing questions, or even right now. Choose one that no one has completely answered yet, and keep it in your mind during your second reading. If you still have the question after reading, continue to think about it—you picked a real keeper!

Your keeper question:

_____

_____

_____

Into Reading

Asking Questions

Asking questions is an important part of understanding what you're reading. Read the following three passages from the story and write a question that you have about each one. Remember your questions as you read the story a second time.

Your questions might be about:

- Why a character does or says something

- Why something happens the way that it does

- What a word, phrase, or sentence means

- A place where you feel confused about what is happening

Passage 1 (page 20)

Juan was stunned. It was one thing for Doña Josefa to go around helping people, but how could she go around handing out gold coins—*his gold coins*?

Your question after reading this passage:

_____

_____

_____

_____

_____

Continue ⟶

Passage 2 (page 24)

The next morning, Juan was up at daybreak. Bathed in the soft dawn light, the mountains seemed to smile at him. When Don Teodosio offered him a lift on horseback, Juan found it difficult to have to say goodbye.

Your question after reading this passage:

_____

_____

_____

Passage 3 (page 25)

"But none of them would take [the gold coin," Doña Josefa said.]
"They all said, 'Keep it. There must be someone who needs it more.' "
  Juan did not say a word.
  "You must be the one who needs it," Doña Josefa said.

Your question after reading this passage:

_____

_____

_____

HEAD in the Clouds

Use your imagination! Choose one of the topics in the clouds and draw a picture or write a little more about the story.

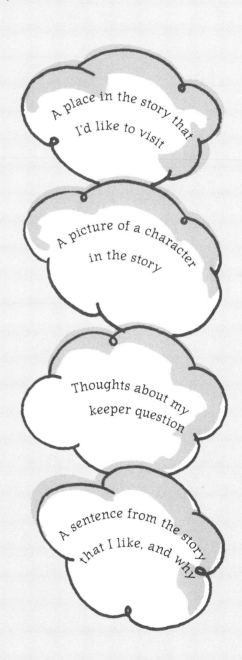

A place in the story that I'd like to visit

A picture of a character in the story

Thoughts about my keeper question

A sentence from the story that I like, and why

Building Your Answer

The focus question:

_____

_____

_____

Your answer to the focus question:

_____

_____

_____

Your answer after the discussion (you may change or add to your first answer):

_____

_____

_____

_____

To support your answer, write one piece of evidence from the story in your own words.

Your evidence:

_____

_____

_____

Prewriting Notes

Write your answer after the discussion from the Building Your Answer page (page 15) in the large box. Then, in the other boxes, write details from the story that support your idea.

Main Idea:

_____

_____

_____

_____

_____

_____

_____

_____

_____

Writing to Explain
Introducing Your Evidence

Evidence:

_____

_____

_____

_____

page _____

Evidence:

_____

_____

_____

_____

page _____

Evidence:

_____

_____

_____

_____

page _____

Writing to Explain
Introducing Your Evidence

Writing a Draft

Write a paragraph based on your prewriting notes (pages 16-17). Use what you wrote in the large box as your main idea and the evidence in the other boxes as support for your main idea. Remember to turn your ideas into complete, detailed sentences.

_____

_____

_____

_____

_____

_____

_____

_____

_____

_____

_____

_____

_____

_____

_____

_____

Writing to Explore
A Plan for Helping

Prewriting Notes

In the left-hand column below, write about someone or something you would like to help. In the right-hand column, write about how your work would help you.

My Plan for Helping _____   **How My Work Will Help Me**

First I will

_____   _____

_____   _____

_____   _____

Then I will

_____   _____

_____   _____

_____   _____

Here are some more things I will do:

_____   _____

_____   _____

_____   _____

_____   _____

Writing to Explore
A Plan for Helping

Writing a Draft

What would be your favorite part of helping other people?

_____

_____

_____

_____

_____

_____

_____

_____

_____

_____

Tuesday of the Other June

by Norma Fox Mazer

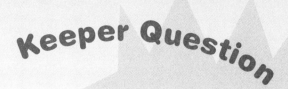

Keeper Question

In the space below, write a keeper question about the story that came into your mind during the first reading, while sharing questions, or even right now. Choose one that no one has completely answered yet, and keep it in your mind during your second reading. If you still have the question after reading, continue to think about it—you picked a real keeper!

Your keeper question:

_____

_____

_____

_____

Into Reading

Asking Questions

Asking questions is an important part of understanding what you're reading. Read the following three passages from the story and write a question that you have about each one. Remember your questions as you read the story a second time.

Your questions might be about:

• Why a character does or says something

• Why something happens the way that it does

• What a word, phrase, or sentence means

• A place where you feel confused about what is happening

Passage 1 (page 33)

I didn't know what to do about her. She was training me like a dog. After a few weeks of this, she only had to look at me, only had to growl, "I'm going to get you, Fish Eyes," for my heart to slink like a whipped dog down into my stomach. My arms were covered with bruises. When my mother noticed, I made up a story about tripping on the sidewalk.

Your question after reading this passage:

_____

_____

_____

_____

_____

Continue ⟶

Into Reading

Asking Questions

Passage 2 (page 34)

Be good, be good, be good, it's just us two women alone in the world . . .
Oh, but if it weren't, if my father wasn't long gone, if we'd had someone else
to fall back on, if . . .

Your question after reading this passage:

_____

_____

_____

_____

Passage 3 (page 40)

I pressed my lips together, clapped my hands over my ears, but without
hope. Wasn't it only a matter of time before I said the hateful words [that the
Other June wanted me to say]?
"How was school?" my mother said that night.
"Okay."

Your question after reading this passage:

_____

_____

_____

_____

HEAD in the Clouds

Use your imagination! Choose one of the topics in the clouds and draw a picture or write a little more about the story.

Something that the story reminds me of

A picture of a character in the story

Thoughts about my keeper question

A note to someone who has bullied me

Building Your Answer

The focus question:

_____

_____

_____

Your answer before the discussion:

_____

_____

_____

Your answer after the discussion (you may change or add to your first answer):

_____

_____

Write down an idea you heard in discussion that is different from yours.

Your classmate's idea:

_____

_____

_____

Writing to Explain
A Letter to Your Classmate

Prewriting Notes

Read your partner's Building Your Answer page for the story "Tuesday of the Other June" (page 26). Ask questions that will help your partner add more to his or her answer and help you understand it better. For example:

- *What do you mean when you say that?*

- *Can you tell me more about the part you mention here?*

- *What things helped you change your answer from before the discussion?*

In the space below, take notes on what your partner tells you about his or her essay. Then switch roles so your partner gets to ask questions.

Your notes on the conversation:

_____

_____

_____

_____

_____

_____

_____

_____

_____

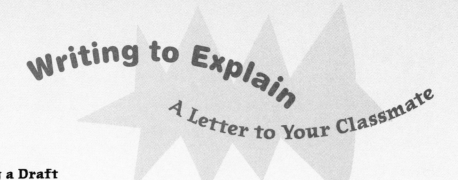

Writing to Explain
A Letter to Your Classmate

Writing a Draft

Write a letter to your partner below. Tell your partner what you learned about his or her answer from your conversation.

A Letter to Your Partner

Dear _____ ,

I learned that you think _____

_____

_____

_____

_____

_____ .

Your answers to my questions helped me see that _____

_____

_____

_____

_____

_____ .

Sincerely,

_____

Writing to Explore
Advice to Remember

Prewriting Notes

Record some advice you remember getting.

Advice About Behaving at Home

1. _____

_____

2. _____

_____

Advice About School and Homework

1. _____

_____

2. _____

_____

Advice About Getting Along with Others

1. _____

_____

2. _____

_____

Writing to Explore
Advice to Remember

Writing a Draft

Using your prewriting notes, make a sign listing the best pieces of advice you've heard from different people. For each piece of advice, include who gave you the advice and why it should be followed. For example: *My mom says if I eat vegetables, then I will grow up to be strong.* If you have time, decorate your sign.

Advice to Remember

1. _____

_____

_____

2. _____

_____

_____

3. _____

_____

_____

Prot and Krot

Polish folktale as told by Agnes Szudek

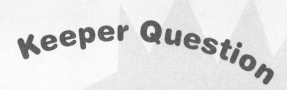

Keeper Question

In the space below, write a keeper question about the story that came into your mind during the first reading, while sharing questions, or even right now. Choose one that no one has completely answered yet, and keep it in your mind during your second reading. If you still have the question after reading, continue to think about it—you picked a real keeper!

Your keeper question:

_____

_____

_____

_____

Connecting your knowledge and personal experience to a story helps you make better sense of the story.

Look in the story for places where you marked a **C**. Below, use your own words to describe what happened in the story. Then explain how that part of the story **connects** to something in your own life.

Something that happens in the story:

_____

_____

_____

_____

_____

_____ **page** _____

Your personal connection to what happens in the story:

_____

_____

_____

_____

_____

Continue ⟶

Into Reading

Making Connections

Something that happens in the story:

_____

_____

_____

_____

_____ **page** _____

Your personal connection to what happens in the story:

_____

_____

_____

_____

HEAD in the Clouds

Use your imagination! Choose one of the topics in the clouds and draw a picture or write a little more about the story.

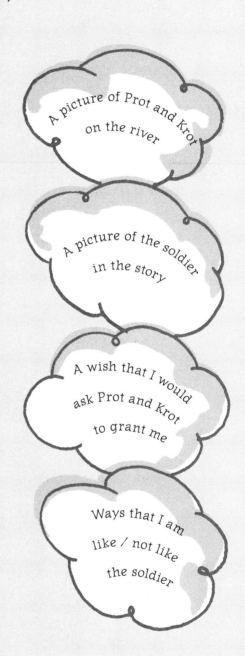

A picture of Prot and Krot on the river

A picture of the soldier in the story

A wish that I would ask Prot and Krot to grant me

Ways that I am like / not like the soldier

Building Your Answer

The focus question:

_____

_____

_____

_____

Your answer before the discussion:

_____

_____

_____

_____

Your answer after the discussion (you may change or add to your first answer):

_____

_____

_____

_____

_____

Writing to Explain
Saying It in Your Own Words

Write down a short passage from "Prot and Krot" that you like:

Passage from page _____:

_____

_____

_____

_____

_____

Now **paraphrase** the passage—retell the passage in your own words:

_____

_____

_____

_____

_____

Writing to Explore
A Clever Wish

Prewriting Notes

Write about a problem you wish to solve.

A problem to solve: _____

_____

_____

Now write about some clever wishes that might help solve the problem.

1. _____

_____

2. _____

_____

3. _____

_____

Circle one of your wishes to write more about.

Some ways the wish you circled might solve the problem: _____

_____

_____

_____

Writing to Explore
A Clever Wish

Writing a Draft

Now write a paragraph about your problem and the wish that would solve your problem. Be sure to explain your problem and solution in complete, detailed sentences.

My Wish

The problem I'd like to solve is _____

_____

_____

_____

One way to solve this problem is to wish for _____

_____

_____

_____

Here's how the wish would solve the problem: _____

_____

_____

_____

_____

Chin Yu Min and the Ginger Cat

by Jennifer Armstrong

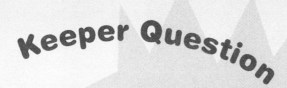

Keeper Question

In the space below, write a keeper question about the story that came into your mind during the first reading, while sharing questions, or even right now. Choose one that no one has completely answered yet, and keep it in your mind during your second reading. If you still have the question after reading, continue to think about it—you picked a real keeper!

Your keeper question:

_____

_____

_____

_____

Into Reading
Making Connections

Connecting your knowledge and personal experience to a story helps you make better sense of the story.

Look in the story for places where you marked a **C**. Below, use your own words to describe what happened in the story. Then explain how that part of the story **connects** to something in your own life.

Something that happens in the story:

_____

_____

_____

_____

_____

_____ page _____

Your personal connection to what happens in the story:

_____

_____

_____

_____

_____

_____

Continue ⟶

Into Reading
Making Connections

Something that happens in the story:

_____

_____

_____

_____

_____

_____ _page_ _____

Your personal connection to what happens in the story:

_____

_____

_____

_____

_____

HEAD in the Clouds

Use your imagination! Choose one of the topics in the clouds and draw a picture or write a little more about the story.

A picture of the ginger cat

What I would draw on a scroll for my house

A sentence from the story that I like, and why

A wise decision that I've made

Building Your Answer

The focus question:

_____

_____

_____

Your answer before the discussion:

_____

_____

_____

Your answer after the discussion (you may change or add to your first answer):

_____

_____

_____

To support your answer, write two pieces of evidence from the story in your own words.

Your evidence:

1. _____

_____

2. _____

_____

Writing to Explain
Explaining Your Evidence

Prewriting Notes

Write your answer after the discussion from the Building Your Answer page (page 47) in the large box. Then complete the web. Remember to explain how your evidence supports the main idea.

Main Idea:

_____

_____

_____

_____

_____

_____

_____

_____

Writing to Explain
Explaining Your Evidence

Evidence:

_____

_____

_____

_____ page

Explanation:

_____

_____

_____

_____

Evidence:

_____

_____

_____

_____ page

Explanation:

_____

_____

_____

_____

Evidence:

_____

_____

_____

_____ page

Explanation:

_____

_____

_____

_____

Writing to Explain
Explaining Your Evidence

Writing a Draft

Now write your essay using your prewriting notes, explaining how your evidence supports your main idea. Give your essay an interesting title.

_____

_____

_____

_____

_____

_____

_____

_____

_____

_____

_____

_____

_____

Writing to Explain
Explaining Your Evidence

Use this page if you need more room.

_____

_____

_____

_____

_____

_____

_____

_____

_____

_____

_____

_____

_____

_____

_____

_____

_____

_____

_____

Writing to Explore
Scrolls for Your Door

Prewriting Notes

In the center box of each web, write a common activity or event. Then write a word that describes that activity in each of the surrounding five boxes.

Scrolls For My Door

Using your prewriting notes, create some scrolls that describe everyday activities. Decorate them if you wish.

The Nightingale

by Hans Christian Andersen

Keeper Question

In the space below, write a keeper question about the story that came into your mind during the first reading, while sharing questions, or even right now. Choose one that no one has completely answered yet, and keep it in your mind during your second reading. If you still have the question after reading, continue to think about it—you picked a real keeper!

Your keeper question:

Into Reading

Making Connections

Connecting your knowledge and personal experience to a story helps you make better sense of the story.

Look in the story for places where you marked a **C**. Below, use your own words to describe what happened in the story. Then explain how that part of the story **connects** to something in your own life.

Something that happens in the story:

_____

_____

_____

_____

_____

_____ *page* _____

Your personal connection to what happens in the story:

_____

_____

_____

_____

_____

Continue ⟶

Into Reading

Making Connections

Something that happens in the story:

_____

_____

_____

_____

_____

_____ page _____

Your personal connection to what happens in the story:

_____

_____

_____

_____

_____

HEAD in the Clouds

Use your imagination! Choose one of the topics in the clouds and draw a picture or write a little more about the story.

A picture of the mechanical nightingale

A note to the Emperor

The words to a nightingale's song

A map of the Emperor's palace and gardens

Building Your Answer

The focus question:

_____

_____

_____

Your answer before the discussion:

_____

_____

_____

Your answer after the discussion _(you may change or add to your first answer):_

_____

_____

_____

_____

An answer you heard in discussion that is different from yours:

_____

_____

_____

_____

Writing to Explain
A Strong Introduction

Prewriting Notes

Use the web below to record your answer after discussion from the Building Your Answer page (page 61). Then record evidence and explain how each piece of evidence supports your answer. Your answer will be the main idea of your essay. Then you'll be ready to write your introduction.

Main Idea:

_____

_____

_____

_____

_____

_____

_____

_____

Writing to Explain
A Strong Introduction

Evidence:

_____
_____
_____
_____
_____ **page** _____

Explanation:

_____
_____
_____
_____

Evidence:

_____
_____
_____
_____
_____ **page** _____

Explanation:

_____
_____
_____
_____

Evidence:

_____
_____
_____
_____
_____ **page** _____

Explanation:

_____
_____
_____
_____

Writing to Explain
A Strong Introduction

Prewriting Notes

An *introduction* to an essay should get the reader's attention with a strong opening sentence; introduce the reader to your main idea; and explain how you are going to support your main idea.

Your opening sentence:

_____

_____

Now write the rest of your introduction, briefly explaining your main idea and what evidence you will use to support your main idea.

Main idea: _____

_____

_____

_____

How you are going to support your main idea: _____

_____

_____

_____

Writing a Draft

Now you are ready to draft your essay, beginning with the introduction you wrote on the facing page. Use your completed web on pages 62–63 to explain in clear, detailed sentences how your evidence supports your main idea (the *body* of your essay).

_____

_____

_____

_____

_____

_____

_____

_____

_____

_____

_____

_____

_____

Writing to Explain
A Strong Introduction

Use this page if you need more room.

_____

_____

_____

_____

_____

_____

_____

_____

_____

_____

_____

_____

_____

_____

_____

_____

_____

_____

Writing to Explore
The Emperor's Palace News

Prewriting Notes

Pretend you are one of the characters from "The Nightingale." Interview your partner using the questions below. Then switch roles.

Your partner's name: _____

Interview Questions

1. *Who* are you? Tell me about yourself.

_____

_____

_____

2. *What* important event did you see today?

_____

_____

_____

_____

3. *When* and *where* did this event happen?

_____

_____

_____

Continue ⟶

Writing to Explore

The Emperor's Palace News

4. Please tell me a little more about what you saw, heard, and felt.

_____

_____

_____

_____

_____

_____

5. _Why_ do you think this event is important? _Why_ do you think it happened?

_____

_____

_____

_____

_____

_____

Writing a Draft

Using the answers your partner gave you, write your newspaper article below. Give it a catchy headline so that people will want to read more.

The Emperor's Palace News

_____

By _____

_____

_____

_____

_____

_____

_____

_____

_____

_____

_____

Writing to Explore

The Emperor's Palace News

Use this page if you need more room.

_____

_____

_____

_____

_____

_____

_____

_____

_____

_____

_____

_____

_____

_____

_____

_____

_____

_____

Fresh

by Philippa Pearce

Keeper Question

In the space below, write a keeper question about the story that came into your mind during the first reading, while sharing questions, or even right now. Choose one that no one has completely answered yet, and keep it in your mind during the second reading. If you still have the question after reading, continue to think about it—you picked a real keeper!

Your keeper question:

_____

_____

_____

_____

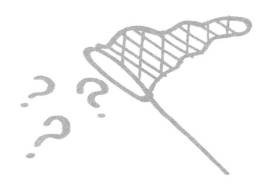

Into Reading
Learning to Visualize

Visualizing helps you create pictures in your mind as you read a story. These pictures could come from your feelings or from any of your five senses (seeing, hearing, touching, tasting, or smelling).

In the space below, write a passage you marked with a **V**. Then describe what you visualize when you read it.

A passage you marked with a V:

_____

_____

_____

_____

_____

_____ page _____

What you visualize while reading:

_____

_____

_____

_____

HEAD in the Clouds

Use your imagination! Choose one of the topics in the clouds and draw a picture or write a little more about the story.

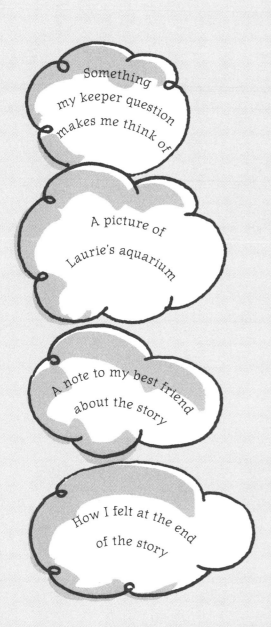

Something my keeper question makes me think of

A picture of Laurie's aquarium

A note to my best friend about the story

How I felt at the end of the story

Building Your Answer

The focus question:

_____

_____

_____

_____

Your answer before the discussion:

_____

_____

_____

_____

Your answer after the discussion _(you may change or add to your first answer)_:

_____

_____

_____

_____

_____

Writing to Explain
Concluding an Essay

Prewriting Notes

Use the web below to write down your main idea and supporting evidence from your Building Your Answer page (page 76). Then you'll be ready to write your introduction and your conclusion.

Main Idea:

_____

_____

_____

_____

_____

_____

_____

_____

Writing to Explain
Concluding an Essay

Evidence:

_____
_____
_____
_____
page _____

Explanation:

_____
_____
_____
_____

Evidence:

_____
_____
_____
_____
page _____

Explanation:

_____
_____
_____
_____

Evidence:

_____
_____
_____
page _____

Explanation:

_____
_____
_____
_____

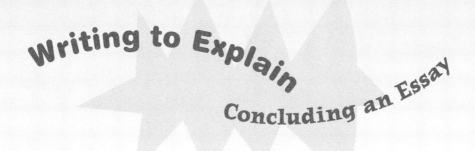

Writing to Explain
Concluding an Essay

Prewriting Notes

Use your web to help you write an *introduction* to your essay. Turn to page 64 for more help.

Your introduction:

_____

_____

_____

_____

_____

Your essay's *conclusion* should remind readers of your answer to the focus question and explain why your idea is important to understanding the story. Practice writing a conclusion below.

Your conclusion:

I think _____

_____

_____

This is important to understanding the story because _____

_____

_____

Writing a Draft

Now you are ready to draft your essay, beginning with the introduction and ending with the conclusion you wrote on the previous page. You can use the web on pages 76–77 to explain how your evidence supports your main idea in clear, detailed sentences.

_____

_____

_____

_____

_____

_____

_____

_____

_____

_____

_____

_____

Writing to Explain
Concluding an Essay

Use this page if you need more room.

_____

_____

_____

_____

_____

_____

_____

_____

_____

_____

_____

_____

_____

_____

_____

_____

_____

_____

Prewriting Notes

Write a story about Laurie and Fresh. First, write the events of your story below, in the order that they will happen. Then write some details about each event. You can describe characters, places, things, or actions important to each event—explaining how things might look, feel, sound, smell, or taste.

My story will be about:

☐ Laurie's train trip with Fresh

☐ Fresh's new home in Laurie's aquarium

First, _____

_____

_____

Details:

1. _____

_____

2. _____

_____

3. _____

_____

Continue ⟶

Writing to Explore

A Story about Fresh

Next, _____

_____

_____

Details:

1. _____

_____

2. _____

_____

3. _____

_____

Writing to Explore
A Story about Fresh

Finally, _____

_____

_____

Details:

1. _____

_____

2. _____

_____

3. _____

_____

Writing to Explore
A Story about Fresh

Writing a Draft

Using your notes, write your story about Fresh below. Your story should have a beginning, middle, and end, as well as a catchy title.

_____

Writing to Explore
A Story about Fresh

Use this page if you need more room.

_____

_____

_____

_____

_____

_____

_____

_____

_____

_____

_____

_____

_____

_____

_____

_____

_____

Thunder, Elephant, and Dorobo

African folktale as told by Humphrey Harman

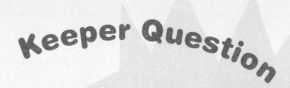
Keeper Question

In the space below, write a keeper question about the story that came into your mind during the first reading, while sharing questions, or even right now. Choose one that no one has completely answered yet, and keep it in your mind during your second reading. If you still have the question after reading, continue to think about it—you picked a real keeper!

Your keeper question:

_____

_____

_____

_____

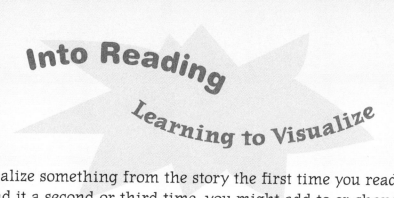

Into Reading
Learning to Visualize

You may visualize something from the story the first time you read it, but when you read it a second or third time, you might add to or change your mental image.

In the space below, write down the page and paragraph numbers of a passage you marked with a **V**. Write a description of what you visualize while reading it.

Your passage: page _____, paragraph _____.

What you visualize while reading this passage:

_____

_____

_____

_____

_____

_____ **page** _____

Now read the passage a second time. Add more details to your original description, or explain how your visualization changed.

How your visualization changed: _____

_____

_____

_____

HEAD in the Clouds

Use your imagination! Choose one of the topics in the clouds and draw a picture or write a little more about the story.

My favorite character in the story

A note telling Thunder why he should not be afraid of Dorobo

A picture of Dorobo

The character that is most like me, and why

Building Your Answer

The focus question:

_____

_____

_____

Your answer before the discussion:

_____

_____

_____

Your answer after the discussion *(you may change or add to your first answer)*:

_____

_____

_____

_____

A quote or a brief passage from the story that supports your answer:

_____

_____

_____

_____

Writing to Explain
A Developed Essay

Prewriting Notes

Fill in the evidence web using your Building Your Answer page (page 91). Then, on pages 94–95, take some notes that will lead to writing an introduction and a conclusion for your essay.

Main Idea:

Writing to Explain
A Developed Essay

Evidence:

_____
_____
_____
_____
_____ *page* _____

Explanation:

_____
_____
_____
_____
_____

Evidence:

_____
_____
_____
_____
_____ *page* _____

Explanation:

_____
_____
_____
_____

Evidence:

_____
_____
_____
_____ *page* _____

Explanation:

_____
_____
_____
_____

Writing to Explain
A Developed Essay

Prewriting Notes

Use your web to help you write an introduction and a conclusion.

Ideas for an Introduction:

_____

_____

_____

_____

_____

_____

_____

Ideas for a Conclusion:

_____

_____

_____

_____

_____

_____

Writing to Explain
A Developed Essay

Writing a Draft

Use the web and your notes (pages 92–94) to write your essay. Each paragraph should contain one piece of evidence and its explanation. Also include an introduction and a conclusion. Give your essay a title that will capture the reader's attention.

_____

_____

_____

_____

_____

_____

_____

_____

_____

_____

_____

_____

_____

_____

_____

Writing to Explain
A Developed Essay

Use this page if you need more room.

_____

_____

_____

_____

_____

_____

_____

_____

_____

_____

_____

_____

_____

_____

_____

_____

Writing to Explore

A Folktale

Prewriting Notes

Choose a thing from nature to write a folk tale about:_____.

These questions might help you think of important features:

Where can the thing you chose be found?	What does it act like?
What does the thing look like? Sound like?	Does it have friends or enemies?

Now write down some important features about the natural thing.

_____

_____

_____

_____

_____

Circle the feature you would like to write your **why** or **how** question about. This is the question you will answer in your folktale.

Now write your **why** or **how** question.

Example: Why is thunder in the sky?

_____

On the next page, make some notes about the beginning, middle, and end of your folktale.

Writing to Explore

A Folktale

Your tale's *beginning* (how things used to be)

Example: Thunder, Elephant, and Dorobo live together on Earth.

_____

_____

_____

_____

Your tale's *middle* (a problem or a change and what happens because of it)

Example: Thunder is afraid of Dorobo and leaves the Earth.

_____

_____

_____

_____

Your tale's *end* (how things are now because of what happened)

Example: Thunder lives in the sky.

_____

_____

_____

_____

Writing to Explore

A Folktale

Writing a Draft

Using your notes, write your folktale in the space below.

The Tale of _____

> Here are some ways to introduce each part of your folktale.
>
> **Beginning:** In the beginning **or** Long ago
>
> **Middle:** Then one day **or** At that moment
>
> **End:** So from then on **or** And that is why

_____

_____

_____

_____

_____

_____

_____

_____

_____

Continue ⟶

Writing to Explore

A Folktale

Use this page if you need more room.

_____

_____

_____

_____

_____

_____

_____

_____

_____

_____

_____

_____

_____

_____

_____

_____

All Summer in a Day

Ray Bradbury

Keeper Question

In the space below, write a keeper question about the story that came into your mind during the first reading, while sharing questions, or even right now. Choose one that no one has completely answered yet, and keep it in your mind during your second reading. If you still have the question after reading, continue to think about it—you picked a real keeper!

Your keeper question:

_____

_____

_____

_____

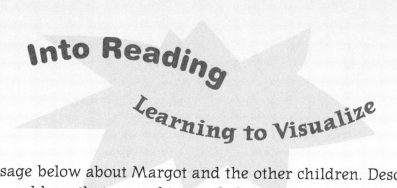

Into Reading
Learning to Visualize

Read the passage below about Margot and the other children. Describe what you visualize and how that mental image helps you understand her feelings.

Passage from the story (page 118):

    If they tagged her and ran, [Margot] stood blinking after them and did not follow. When the class sang songs about happiness and life and games, her lips barely moved. Only when they sang about the sun and the summer did her lips move as she watched the drenched windows.

What you visualize when you read this passage: _____

_____

_____

_____

How you think Margot might feel in this passage: _____

_____

_____

_____

A memory from your own life that helps you understand how Margot feels:

_____

_____

_____

_____

_____

HEAD in the Clouds

Use your imagination! Choose one of the topics in the clouds and draw a picture or write a little more about the story.

A note to Margot

Something I would do if it rained all day

The moment the sun comes out on Venus

My own short poem about the sun

Building Your Answer

The focus question:

_____

_____

_____

Your answer before the discussion:

_____

_____

_____

Your answer after the discussion (you may change or add to your first answer):

_____

_____

_____

_____

An answer you heard in discussion that is different from yours:

_____

_____

_____

_____

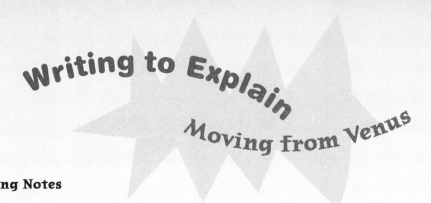

Writing to Explain
Moving from Venus

Prewriting Notes

To write an essay convincing people to move from Venus, you will need to give your readers good reasons. First, write some reasons people might have for living on Venus. Then write some convincing reasons for moving from Venus. Where you can, support your ideas with evidence from the story.

Reasons to live on Venus:

1. _____

_____

2. _____

_____

3. _____

_____

Reasons to move from Venus:

1. _____

_____

2. _____

_____

3. _____

_____

Writing to Explain
Moving from Venus

Writing a Draft

Using your prewriting notes, draft your essay below. Remember, you are writing to make people want to move from Venus. Give the reasons that people might want to live on Venus, and then explain why your reasons for moving from Venus are more convincing.

_____

_____

_____

_____

_____

_____

_____

_____

_____

_____

_____

_____

_____

_____

Writing to Explain
Moving from Venus

Use this page if you need more room.

_____

_____

_____

_____

_____

_____

_____

_____

_____

_____

_____

_____

_____

_____

_____

_____

Writing to Explore
A Summer Poem

Prewriting Notes

In the chart below, list some of your favorite summer experiences.

Places to Go	Things to Do	Foods to Eat
_____	_____	_____
_____	_____	_____
_____	_____	_____
_____	_____	_____
_____	_____	_____
_____	_____	_____
_____	_____	_____

Continue ⟶

Writing to Explore

A Summer Poem

From your chart on the previous page, choose one experience from each column that you would like to write about in your poem. Write about each experience in more detail below.

(Place to go)	(Thing to do)	(Food to eat)
Details:	**Details:**	**Details:**

Describing in Detail

Need help thinking of details? Think about these questions as you write:

- Where does this experience happen? Who enjoys it with me?

- How does this experience make me feel?

- How does it taste? Sound? Smell? What does it look like?

Writing to Explore

A Summer Poem

Writing a Draft

Now write your poem about summer in three stanzas, using your prewriting notes.

_____

_____

_____

_____

_____

_____

_____

_____

_____

_____

_____

_____

_____

_____

Beauty and the Beast

Madame de Villeneuve

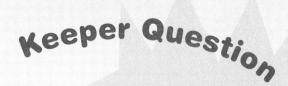

Keeper Question

In the space below, write a keeper question about the story that came into your mind during the first reading, while sharing questions, or even right now. Choose one that no one has completely answered yet, and keep it in your mind during your second reading. If you still have the question after reading, continue to think about it—you picked a real keeper!

Your keeper question:

_____

_____

_____

_____

Into Reading
Putting It All Together

You have practiced asking **questions**, making **connections**, and **visualizing** during your first reading of this story. Look back at your notes and choose one passage you marked with a **?**, one you marked with a **C**, and one you marked with a **V**. Below, explain how you used each strategy.

The passage marked with a **?** is on page _____, paragraph _____.

Your question about this passage: _____

_____

_____

_____

The passage marked with a **C** is on page _____, paragraph _____.

Your connection to this passage: _____

_____

_____

_____

The passage marked with a **V** is on page _____, paragraph _____.

What you visualize while reading this passage: _____

_____

_____

_____

HEAD in the Clouds

Use your imagination! Choose one of the topics in the clouds and draw a picture or write a little more about the story.

What the Beast looks like

A picture of the Beast's castle

Something in the story that I am curious about

Why I like or don't like this story

Building Your Answer

The focus question:

_____

_____

_____

Your answer before the discussion:

_____

_____

_____

Your answer after the discussion (you may change or add to your first answer):

_____

_____

_____

Evidence from the story / something from discussion (circle one) **that supports your answer:**

_____

_____

_____

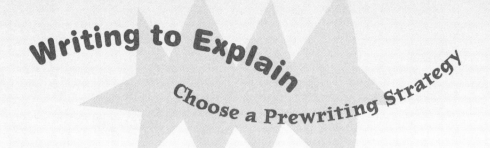

Writing to Explain

Choose a Prewriting Strategy

Prewriting Notes

Look at the Building Your Answer page on page 119. Then make a
list / web / chart (circle one) that shows:

• Your answer (the main idea)

• Evidence from the story that supports your answer, told in your own words

• How your evidence supports your answer

Writing a Draft

Write your essay, using your prewriting notes, in the space below.

_____

_____

_____

_____

_____

_____

_____

_____

_____

_____

_____

_____

_____

_____

_____

_____

_____

_____

Writing to Explain
Choose a Prewriting Strategy

Use this page if you need more room.

_____

_____

_____

_____

_____

_____

_____

_____

_____

_____

_____

_____

_____

_____

_____

Writing to Explore
Your Dream Palace

Prewriting Notes

Choose three important things about your dream palace that you would like to include in a description. Write some important details about each feature—think about what you see, hear, smell, taste, and feel in your dream palace.

Feature 1: _____

Details: _____

_____

_____

_____

_____

Feature 2: _____

Details: _____

_____

_____

_____

_____

Continue ⟶

Writing to Explore
Your Dream Palace

Feature 3: _____

Details: _____

_____

_____

_____

_____

How my dream palace shows the kind of person I am:

_____

_____

_____

_____

_____

_____

_____

_____

_____

Writing a Draft

Now write about your dream palace using your prewriting notes. Start a new paragraph for each topic. Your last paragraph should explain what your dream palace shows about you.

My Dream Palace

_____

_____

_____

_____

_____

_____

_____

_____

_____

_____

_____

_____

_____

Writing to Explore
Your Dream Palace

Use this page if you need more room.

_____

_____

_____

_____

_____

_____

_____

_____

_____

_____

_____

_____

_____

_____

Writing Notebook

This is your chance to look back at what you have written in your Reader's Journal, choose a piece you wrote that you like, and make it the best it can be. Here's how to revise your draft:

1. Choose the Writing to Explain piece you wrote that you would most like to revise.

2. Mark the page with a paper clip or a sticky note and turn in your Reader's Journal to your teacher. Your teacher will write a question or note on the planning page (page 130, 134, or 138) for you to think about.

3. Read and think about your teacher's note. Review the story and your Reader's Journal for more ideas.

4. Plan your revised writing in the prewriting notes section (page 131, 135, or 139). Then write your revised draft on the next page.

Writing Notebook
Planning Page

Choose a piece to revise about one of these stories (circle one):

Thank You, M'am   **The Gold Coin**   **Tuesday of the Other June**

It is on page _____ of the Reader's Journal.

Think about your teacher's note to help you make your writing shine.

_____ **Make your main idea clearer.**

Teacher's note: _____

_____

_____

_____ **Give more evidence to support your main idea.**

Teacher's note: _____

_____

_____

_____ **Explain more about how your evidence supports the main idea.**

Teacher's note: _____

_____

_____

Writing Notebook
Planning Page

Prewriting Notes

Use a web, a chart, or a list to plan your writing.

Writing Notebook

Final Draft

Writing Notebook
Final Draft

Use this page if you need more room.

_____

_____

_____

_____

_____

_____

_____

_____

_____

_____

_____

_____

_____

_____

_____

_____

_____

Writing Notebook
Planning Page

Choose a piece to revise about one of these stories (circle one):

Prot and Krot   **Chin Yu Min and the Ginger Cat**   **The Nightingale**

It is on page _____ of the Reader's Journal.

Think about your teacher's note to help you make your writing shine.

_____ **Give more evidence to support a main idea.**

Teacher's note: _____

_____

_____

_____ **Paraphrase story events to use as evidence.**

Teacher's note: _____

_____

_____

_____ **Make your introduction state your main idea and how you will support it.**

Teacher's note: _____

_____

_____

_____ **Make your introduction more catchy to get your reader's attention.**

Teacher's note: _____

_____

_____

Writing Notebook
Planning Page

Prewriting Notes

Use a web, a chart, or a list to plan your writing.

Writing Notebook
Final Draft

_____

_____

_____

_____

_____

_____

_____

_____

_____

_____

_____

_____

_____

_____

_____

_____

_____

Writing Notebook
Final Draft

Use this page if you need more room.

_____

_____

_____

_____

_____

_____

_____

_____

_____

_____

_____

_____

_____

_____

_____

_____

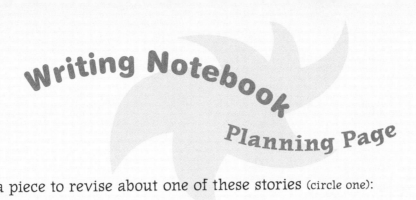

Writing Notebook
Planning Page

Choose a piece to revise about one of these stories (circle one):

Fresh   **Thunder, Elephant, and Dorobo**

All Summer in a Day   **Beauty and the Beast**

It is on page _____ of the Reader's Journal.

Think about your teacher's note to help you make your writing shine.

_____ **Make your conclusion restate your answer to the focus question.**

Teacher's note: _____

_____

_____

_____ **Make your conclusion say how your answer helps you understand the story.**

Teacher's note: _____

_____

_____

_____ **Make sure to explain how each piece of evidence supports the main idea.**

Teacher's note: _____

_____

_____

_____ **Give more evidence from the story to explain the main idea.**

Teacher's note: _____

_____

Prewriting Notes

Use a web, a chart, or a list to plan your writing.

Writing Notebook
Final Draft

_____

_____
_____
_____
_____
_____
_____
_____
_____
_____
_____
_____
_____
_____
_____
_____
_____
_____
_____
_____
_____
_____

Writing Notebook
Final Draft

Use this page if you need more room.

_____

_____

_____

_____

_____

_____

_____

_____

_____

_____

_____

_____

_____

_____

_____

_____

_____

_____

Curious Words

For each story, write down a curious word and the page number where the word appears. Then do one of the following:

- Write why you like your curious word, why it seems curious to you, or why you remember it.

- Pretend that one of the characters in the story uses your curious word and write down something the character says.

- Use your curious word in a message—for example, in a birthday or a friendship card, in a poem, or in a funny note to a friend.

- Make up a fun way to use the word yourself.

Curious Words

Thank You, M'am

Your curious word _____ **page** _____

_____

_____

_____

_____

Your curious word _____ **page** _____

_____

_____

_____

_____

Your curious word _____ **page** _____

_____

_____

_____

_____

Curious Words

The Gold Coin

Your curious word _____ **page** _____

_____

_____

_____

_____

Your curious word _____ **page** _____

_____

_____

_____

_____

Your curious word _____ **page** _____

_____

_____

_____

_____

Curious Words

Tuesday of the Other June

Your curious word _____ page _____

_____

_____

_____

_____

Your curious word _____ page _____

_____

_____

_____

_____

Your curious word _____ page _____

_____

_____

_____

_____

Curious Words

Prot and Krot

Your curious word _____ **page** _____

_____

_____

_____

_____

Your curious word _____ **page** _____

_____

_____

_____

_____

Your curious word _____ **page** _____

_____

_____

_____

_____

Curious Words

Chin Yu Min and the Ginger Cat

Your curious word _____ **page** _____

_____

_____

_____

_____

Your curious word _____ **page** _____

_____

_____

_____

_____

Your curious word _____ **page** _____

_____

_____

_____

_____

Curious Words

The Nightingale

Your curious word _____ **page** _____

_____

_____

_____

_____

Your curious word _____ **page** _____

_____

_____

_____

_____

Your curious word _____ **page** _____

_____

_____

_____

_____

Curious Words

Fresh

Your curious word _____ **page** _____

_____

_____

_____

_____

Your curious word _____ **page** _____

_____

_____

_____

_____

Your curious word _____ **page** _____

_____

_____

_____

_____

Curious Words

Thunder, Elephant, and Dorobo

Your curious word _____ **page** _____

_____

_____

_____

_____

Your curious word _____ **page** _____

_____

_____

_____

_____

Your curious word _____ **page** _____

_____

_____

_____

_____

Curious Words

All Summer in a Day

Your curious word _____ **page** _____

_____

_____

_____

_____

Your curious word _____ **page** _____

_____

_____

_____

_____

Your curious word _____ **page** _____

_____

_____

_____

_____

Curious Words

Beauty and the Beast

Your curious word _____ **page** _____

_____

_____

_____

_____

Your curious word _____ **page** _____

_____

_____

_____

_____

Your curious word _____ **page** _____

_____

_____

_____

_____

Glossary

In this glossary, you'll find definitions for words that you may not know, but that are in the stories you've read. You'll find the meaning of each word as it is used in the story. The word may have other meanings as well, which you can find in a dictionary if you're interested. If you don't find a word here that you're wondering about, go to your dictionary for help.

absorbing: Something is **absorbing** if it captures all your attention. The movie was so **absorbing** that no one heard the doorbell ring. If you have an **absorbing** interest in horses, you might read a lot of books about them or learn to ride them.

Abuelo: Spanish for *Grandfather*.

accustomed: When you are **accustomed** to something, you are used to it. You would be **accustomed** to practicing after school if you play on a sports team. If you go to bed every night at nine o'clock, you will become **accustomed** to going to sleep at that time.

adjust: To **adjust** to something is to become more and more comfortable with it. It might take you several weeks to **adjust** to a new school or a new baby in the family. The baseball team had to **adjust** to playing in spring instead of autumn.

adjustment: An **adjustment** is a change you make to get used to something. You would make an **adjustment** to a different way of life if you were to move from the country to the city.

agate: A kind of stone that is striped with different colors. **Agate** is a type of quartz, which is one of the most common minerals found in the earth.

aloof: You are **aloof** when you are cool and distant in manner and when you keep to yourself. The new boy is **aloof**; we're not certain whether he wants to be friends with us.

amiably: If you do something **amiably**, you are pleasant and good-natured when you do it. My neighbor always smiles and responds **amiably** when we say hello to him.

anoraks: An **anorak** is a heavy hooded jacket. **Anoraks** are usually waterproof and very warm.

apparatus: The thing or things used for a particular job or purpose. The equipment in a laboratory is an example of the **apparatus** needed to do a science experiment.

appointed: Something **appointed** has been decided or set. The book club changed their **appointed** meeting date because of bad driving weather.

aromatic: Something is **aromatic** if it has a pleasant smell. A pot of **aromatic** stew cooking on a stove might fill the kitchen with a wonderful scent.

artificial: Something **artificial** is made by human beings instead of occurring in nature. Some people prefer **artificial** flowers to fresh-cut flowers because real flowers don't last as long. My grandfather has an **artificial** hip.

astonished: You are **astonished** when you are surprised or shocked by something because it is so unusual. You might be **astonished** if you saw a pig swim or if your mother served you ice cream for breakfast.

astonishment: To feel **astonishment** is to feel surprise or shock. I stared in **astonishment** when my teacher juggled six tennis balls.

attributed: To **attribute** is to view a certain thing as the cause of something else. The coach **attributed** the team's win to their hard work on the practice field.

aviary: A place where birds are kept.

banished: If you are **banished**, you are sent away from a place and forbidden to come back. The king **banished** the thief from the castle, telling him never to return.

barren: Something is **barren** when it is empty or is missing something. The walls of the abandoned house are **barren**.

befell: Happened to. **Befell** is the past tense of *befall*. No matter what **befell** them, the friends stuck together and helped each other.

beseech: You **beseech** someone when you make a strong request or beg for something. I will **beseech** my teacher for two extra days to do my homework assignment.

blacksmiths: A **blacksmith** is a person who makes horseshoes and other things out of iron. **Blacksmiths** are able to shape iron by heating it over a fire and then hammering it while it is still hot.

blue suede shoes: A style of fancy shoes, popular with teenagers in the 1950s.

blundering: Clumsy. The **blundering** dog knocked over garbage cans and potted plants wherever it went.

brine: Very salty water or seawater.

brooches: A **brooch** is a decorative piece of jewelry you pin onto your clothes. Some **brooches** are made of silver, gold, or other jewels.

captive: Someone or something held prisoner or kept under the control of another. The lion is a **captive** in his cage at the zoo.

carp: A freshwater fish that lives in ponds, lakes, and slow streams.

catastrophe: A complete failure. If it rained the day you went to the amusement park and your car broke down on the way home, you might say the trip was a **catastrophe**.

ceased: To **cease** is to come to an end; to stop. The music suddenly **ceased** and the room was silent.

ceaseless: Nonstop; constant. Days of **ceaseless** sun bleached the fossil bones to a pure white.

chambermaids: A **chambermaid** is a person hired to clean and take care of bedrooms in a house or a hotel.

civil: Well-mannered. You are **civil** when you wait your turn in line and don't push ahead of the people in front of you. Your mother would expect you to be **civil** to guests in your home, even if you don't like them.

clambered: To **clamber** is to climb or move with difficulty, usually on hands and feet. The children **clambered** up the slippery riverbank.

clerks: A **clerk** is a person who keeps track of money and other business matters for another person or a company. The businessman let his **clerks** make all the decisions about what to do with his savings.

commissions: Formal orders or paid requests for something. The artist was given several **commissions** to make sculptures for the new park.

compounded: Things that are **compounded** come together or are combined to make a whole, or they are added together to increase over time. Because she didn't take it easy when she first got sick, the girl's illness was **compounded** and she was absent from school for a week.

concealed: To **conceal** is to hide something. We often **conceal** things we don't want others to know about. The stolen treasure was **concealed** in a box in the attic.

concussion: A sudden, violent crashing or shaking. You can hear and feel the **concussion** of a washing machine when it has too many clothes in it.

considerate: You are **considerate** when you are thoughtful of other people's needs and feelings. A **considerate** person might ask a neighbor how she is feeling when she comes home from the hospital.

courtier: A person who is in the court of a king or queen.

cress: A plant whose leaves can be eaten in salads. **Cress** often has a strong peppery taste.

croon: A soft singing. A **croon** and some gentle rocking might put a baby to sleep.

crossly: You behave **crossly** if you are in a bad mood and act grouchy. You might speak **crossly** if your younger sister were annoying you. People often act **crossly** when they don't feel well.

cultivated: You **cultivate** land when you grow crops on it. You also **cultivate** something when you help it grow. My neighbor **cultivated** lettuce in her garden.

cunningly: Cleverly; with skill. The old magician performed all his card tricks so **cunningly**, we couldn't figure out how he'd done them.

cylinder: A solid or hollow object that is shaped like a can, with curved sides and a circular top and bottom. A telescope is a long, thin **cylinder** with a powerful magnifying glass at one end.

daybed: A couch with a low back.

deceive: You **deceive** people when you make them believe something that isn't true. I tried to **deceive** the school nurse with a fake coughing fit, but she wasn't fooled.

definite: Certain; without doubt. A multiple-choice test question has one **definite** right answer, but an essay question might have more than one right answer. Something is also **definite** when it has exact or fixed limits. You and your friend might set a **definite** time to meet at the corner.

desert, deserted: To **desert** is to go away from someone or something you have a duty to stay with or support. He refused to **desert** his old friends when he became popular. Something **deserted** has been abandoned. The **deserted** prairie was once filled with roaming buffalo.

desolate: When you feel **desolate**, you feel unhappy and lonely at the same time. You would feel **desolate** if your best friend moved away. A lost traveler might look **desolate** walking down the street by himself. A **desolate** place does not have people living there. If your family moves, your old home would be **desolate** until someone else moves in.

determined: Something **determined** is figured out firmly or ahead of time. You might meet your friends at the park at a **determined** time every week.

devoted: To be **devoted** is to give time or attention entirely to someone or something. My friend is **devoted** to chess and won't play any other game.

dignified: Serious, calm, and formal. You might act **dignified** when you receive a special award or prize at school.

dimly: Something seen or felt **dimly** cannot be easily and clearly seen or figured out. The light of the television shone **dimly** through the window of the dark house. You might **dimly** remember visiting the beach when you were three years old.

dint: Force or effort. By **dint** of hard work, the students finished decorating before the party.

direst: Something **dire** is desperate. You would be in **dire** need of water if you were walking in the desert. Of all the towns hit by the earthquake, ours was in the **direst** condition and needed the most help.

dismal: Gloomy or depressing. Weeks of rainy weather had put everyone in a **dismal** mood.

dismay: Shock or loss of courage, often in the face of danger or difficulty. The hikers were in **dismay** to find that the rain made the mountain trail too hard to follow.

dismounted: When you **dismount**, you get off or get down from something. The children **dismounted** their bikes to cross the street.

distressed: To be **distressed** is to feel pain, sorrow, or worry. You would be **distressed** if you found out that your friend had been in an accident. The kitten's disappearance greatly **distressed** the child.

doleful, dolefully: Someone who is **doleful** is very sad or filled with sorrow. The children were **doleful** when the class guinea pig died. The little boy looked **dolefully** at the broken toy, sorry that it had come apart.

Don: A title in Spanish that you use with an older man's first name to show your respect.

Doña: A title in Spanish that you use with an older woman's first name to show your respect.

drenched: You're **drenched** when you're completely wet. Everyone on the playground was **drenched** after the sudden storm. The runners were **drenched** in sweat at the end of the race.

droning: Speaking in a dull tone of voice. **Droning** on and on, the speaker almost put the audience to sleep.

ecstasies: Someone who is in **ecstasies** is feeling great joy or wonder. I was in **ecstasies** over the fish tank my parents gave me for my birthday.

embedding: Something that is **embedding** something else is surrounding it firmly and completely. Fossils are made when the sand or dirt **embedding** small creatures and plants hardens to stone over hundreds of thousands of years.

embers: The hot pieces of coal or wood that are left glowing when a fire burns out. The **embers** of the campfire were slow to fade.

emerging: If something is **emerging**, it is coming into view or coming out of hiding. You know that it's spring when all the flowers start **emerging** from the ground.

enchant: To **enchant** is to charm and delight. The dolphins at the aquarium might **enchant** you with their tricks.

esteemed: If a person is **esteemed**, he or she is someone others respect and have a high opinion of. A teacher whom all students trust and admire might be considered an **esteemed** teacher.

exquisite: Lovely, delicate, or wonderful. The colorful lines and markings on a beetle's wings are **exquisite**.

extravagance: Spending too much money on things you don't really need. Buying a diamond necklace or a private airplane is an act of **extravagance**. Her **extravagance** made her popular with her friends, but she had trouble paying her bills.

fashioned: When you **fashion** something, you form, shape, or create it. The two sisters **fashioned** a fishing pole from a stick and some string.

fatal: Something **fatal** causes death or great harm. The bite of a poisonous snake is **fatal**. You would make a **fatal** mistake if you jumped into the deep end of a pool without knowing how to swim.

ferocious: If a person or animal is **ferocious**, it is cruel, fierce, or violent. After he saw the movie about the **ferocious** monster, he had nightmares about it chasing him and trying to bite him.

forlornly: Someone acting **forlornly** feels sadness for being left alone or lonely. The puppy left out in the rainstorm began to whimper **forlornly** as it grew wetter and wetter.

fortunate: You are **fortunate** if good or lucky things happen to you. I am **fortunate** to have lots of wonderful friends.

frail: Someone **frail** is weak. You might feel **frail** after a long illness.

frisky: Full of energy and playfulness. Whenever my dad puts on salsa music, my brother and I get **frisky** and start to dance.

gaiety: Cheerfulness or joy. Our house is always filled with **gaiety** when we throw a party.

gaping: When you **gape** at something, you stare at it with great surprise and wonder. She stood **gaping** at the sight of the rocket ship lifting off.

good riddance: A way of saying you are glad something you don't like is going away or getting out of your sight. You might say "**Good riddance**!" if you found out your loud, rude neighbors were moving out of the house next door.

grasped: To **grasp** something is to grab it and hold it tightly. My little sister **grasped** my hand so that she wouldn't get separated from me in the crowd.

gratified: If you are **gratified**, you are happy or satisfied because you have gotten something that you wanted. A baby might be **gratified** after having a bottle of milk.

gravely: With great seriousness. The man spoke **gravely** about his time at war.

grieved: To be **grieved** is to feel great sadness. I am always **grieved** to hear news of a fire or an accident.

grimly: If you say something **grimly**, you say it in a very serious, stern, and often unfriendly way. The judge **grimly** told the thief that he was going to jail.

gruff, gruffly: Someone who speaks **gruffly** has a deep and rough-sounding voice. Being **gruff** can also mean that you do things in a harsh or rude manner. My neighbor is very **gruff**; he just frowns at us when we say hello to him.

grumbling: Making a low, deep, rolling sound with no words, like the **grumbling** of a lion before it roars. Also, a person who is **grumbling** is complaining in a low, grouchy tone of voice. She is always **grumbling** about having to take out the trash.

haggled: To **haggle** is to bargain over the price of something. The customer **haggled** with the salesperson to try and get a better deal on the car.

half nelson: A kind of wrestling hold.

haughty: If you are proud of yourself while looking down on others, you are **haughty**. A **haughty** person might brag about a new coat while someone else wears a torn coat. The **haughty** student thought he was smarter than all his classmates.

hence: An old-fashioned way of saying "from now." If you agree to meet your friend two weeks **hence**, that means you would meet her two weeks from that day at the same time.

heron: A **heron** is a type of water bird. **Herons** have long necks and beaks, and very long legs for wading in deep water.

hoisted: You **hoist** something when you lift or pull it up. The mechanical crane **hoisted** heavy pieces of metal and wood into the air.

honorable: Someone who is honest and shows a sense of what is right and proper is **honorable**. You might also call someone **honorable** if you want to show your respect for that person.

hospitality: A friendly and welcoming way of treating people, especially guests or visitors. You might show **hospitality** to new neighbors by inviting them over for dinner.

huddled: You **huddle** by gathering yourself in a tight bundle, either with others or by pulling your arms and legs in against your body. The troop of Boy Scouts **huddled** around a campfire to keep warm.

huffing: Someone is **huffing** if they are breathing or blowing very hard. She was **huffing** by the time she walked all the way up the hill.

icebox: A refrigerator. Before there was electricity, you would have used an **icebox**, which is an insulated cabinet that contains a large block of ice to keep food cold.

illuminated: Something **illuminated** is lit up. During the blackout, the house was **illuminated** by candles. The ocean waves were **illuminated** in the moonlight.

immense: Something is **immense** if it is huge or of great size. An ocean is an **immense** body of water. An avalanche occurs when an **immense** amount of snow suddenly slides down a mountain.

imperial: Having something to do with an emperor or the people and place over which the emperor has power (which is called the *empire*). The emperor loved to walk through the **imperial** gardens during sunrise.

implored: Begged or asked urgently for something. I **implored** my parents to raise my allowance. The prisoner **implored** the judge to let him go free.

impudent: You are **impudent** when you are rude, bold, and disrespectful. If you gave your friend half of your cookies, it would be **impudent** of her to demand more. My **impudent** reply to my uncle got me grounded for a week.

indebted: Feeling grateful to someone who has done you a favor. You would be **indebted** to someone who helped you when you were lost. You are also **indebted** when you owe someone money. Your friend would be **indebted** to you if you loaned him lunch money.

indignantly: If you do or say something **indignantly**, you are upset because you feel that something is not fair. You might stomp off to your room **indignantly** if your parents punished you for something you didn't do.

inferior: If something is **inferior** to something else, it is not as good, important, or valuable. The movie my brother picked to watch was **inferior** to the one I picked last week.

insistent: Firm and repeated. If your sister tells you all afternoon long that she's going to hide your homework, she's making an **insistent** threat. My teacher's **insistent** directions are to read each story twice before discussing it.

insolence: Bold, rude behavior. The people sitting behind us at the movie showed great **insolence** by talking loudly and throwing popcorn.

intention: An **intention** is something that a person plans or decides to do. His **intention** was to drive to his grandparents' house, but his car broke down, so he took the train.

intermixed: To say things are **intermixed** is another way of saying they are mixed together. My closet contains summer clothes and winter clothes, all **intermixed**. We **intermixed** the leftover red and blue paint to make purple.

intricate: If something is **intricate**, it is not simple and often has a lot of parts or pieces. The inside of a computer is an **intricate** system. A very detailed design is often described as **intricate**. The wood clock has an **intricate** carving of birds on the front.

kingfisher: A **kingfisher** is a type of water bird that feeds on fish. **Kingfishers** have large beaks and are usually brightly colored.

kitchenette: A small kitchen.

kowtowed: When you **kowtow** to someone, you kneel in front of him or her with your head touching the ground as a sign of respect.

lackeys: A **lackey** is a servant.

lacquer: A substance that is put on a surface and dries to a very shiny coat. **Lacquer** is used on some types of furniture as well as plates and bowls.

lamented: To **lament** is to express grief, either out loud (crying or moaning) or by just feeling very sad. The children **lamented** the loss of their hamster.

larder: A small room or closet where food is stored.

latching: If you **latch** on to something, you grab and hold it tightly. A sailor might **latch** on to his life preserver if his boat tipped over. The puppy keeps **latching** on to the rope with its teeth and pulling hard.

lateral: On the side or to the side. Most crabs walk using a **lateral** motion instead of going forward.

lattice: A **lattice** is formed when strips of something, like metal or wood, are laid across each other to form a crisscross pattern. Fences sometimes have a **lattice** design. The baker makes apple pies with **lattice** crusts on top.

leagues: A **league** is a measure of length equal to about three miles. A hundred **leagues** is about three hundred miles.

lee: The sheltered side of something. You might climb the **lee** of a hill to avoid the strong wind blowing against the other side of it.

lurking: People or animals who are **lurking** are staying hidden, usually because they are being sneaky or are up to no good. You might **lurk** behind a door so that you can jump out and scare your friend. The cat is **lurking** in the grass, waiting for a mouse to appear.

magnificent: Something **magnificent** is very grand, excellent, or beautiful. The **magnificent** old train station was made out of marble. The trees of a redwood forest are a **magnificent** sight.

mantle: A loose, sleeveless coat. Someone might wear a heavy **mantle** over his clothes in the winter to keep warm.

marvelous: Something that is **marvelous** causes wonder or amazement. There might be a **marvelous** fireworks display on the Fourth of July. Something **marvelous** can also be of excellent or high quality.

mast: A tall pole that stands on the deck of a boat or ship and supports its sails. In some old movies, pirates swing from the **mast** when capturing a ship.

meager: If something is **meager**, there is very little or not enough of it. I feel cranky later in the morning if I eat a **meager** breakfast. The farmer's **meager** harvest of corn was not worth selling at the market.

mechanical: Made or operated by machinery. The garage has a **mechanical** door that opens when you press a button.

melodious: A sound that is **melodious** is pleasant to hear. The sound of a church bell ringing is **melodious**. A good storyteller might have a **melodious** voice.

merriment: Fun and enjoyment. The children giggled with **merriment** as they watched the clowns at the circus.

minnows: A **minnow** is a tiny fish that lives in fresh water.

misfortune, misfortunes: Your **misfortunes** are the unlucky or unhappy things that happen to you. You might have the **misfortune** to get sick during the winter holidays.

mistrusted: Someone who is **mistrusted** is not trusted—you suspect that the person won't do what you want or hope. I have **mistrusted** my friend ever since I found out that he was talking behind my back.

monastery: A **monastery** is a place where monks (religious men) live, work, and study together. Those who live in **monasteries** live very simple lives and don't have many possessions or much money.

mother-of-pearl: The hard, smooth, pearly layer on the inside of certain oyster shells and sea shells. **Mother-of-pearl** is often used to make buttons and jewelry.

mussels: A **mussel** is a type of shellfish. It has a narrow, blue-black shell.

nondescript: If something is **nondescript**, it doesn't have many things about it that make it stand out or easy to describe. One brick of a brick wall would be **nondescript** unless it had something written on it or was a different color.

obliged: You are **obliged** to do something if you have to do it—it is important or you have no choice. If you broke your neighbor's window playing ball, you would be **obliged** to pay for a new window. You could be **obliged** to go back and get your homework assignment if you left it in your desk.

obligingly: When you do something **obligingly**, you do it willingly. Our neighbor **obligingly** helped us carry our groceries in from the car.

octopi: The plural of *octopus*.

odes: An **ode** is a poem written to honor something or someone. The first **odes** were written in ancient Greece, often about warriors, athletes, and other people who had done great or exciting things.

overtook: Caught up with something or someone, sometimes in a sudden or surprising way. **Overtook** is the past tense of *overtake*. When we sped up, our car **overtook** the other cars on the road. Sadness **overtook** me when I learned that my best friend was moving away.

pantomime: A play or scene acted out with movements of the body and face instead of words. A **pantomime** might use music, costumes, and scenery to help make the story clear.

peerless: If something is **peerless**, it is so special and wonderful that it doesn't compare to anyone or anything else. You would say that your grandmother's apple pie is **peerless** if you have never tasted any better apple pie.

pining: When you are **pining**, you are feeling unhappy because you miss something or want something you cannot have. You might spend the winter **pining** for the days when it was sunny and warm outside.

plaited: To **plait** something is to braid it. My mother **plaited** my sister's hair every morning before school.

pondered: You **ponder** when you think carefully about something. You might **ponder** whether you really want to attend a party. He **pondered** the meaning of his odd dream.

ponderously: To do something **ponderously** is to do it in a heavy, slow, and clumsy way. The huge truck moved **ponderously** through the traffic jam. I got up **ponderously** from the couch after I'd fallen asleep watching television.

porcelain: Something made of **porcelain** is made of a kind of pottery that is very thin and hard. Dishes and teacups are sometimes made of **porcelain**, as are fancy dolls.

presentable: When you make something **presentable**, you make it fit to be seen. You might make your house **presentable** if you were having company for dinner. Your mom might also ask you to wear slacks instead of jeans so that you look more **presentable**.

procured: To **procure** something is to get it by making an effort. After reaching and stretching for what seemed like hours, the girl finally **procured** the ball stuck underneath the sofa.

projection: Something that sticks out. A goat's horns are **projections** that grow from the top of its head.

prosperous: People are **prosperous** if they are successful or have wealth. The owner of a neighborhood bank may be **prosperous**. You might hope to build a **prosperous** business when you grow up.

provoked: When you **provoke** someone, you do something to make him or her angry, annoyed, or disturbed. I **provoked** my little sister by kicking her under the table.

prudent: A **prudent** person thinks carefully and uses good sense before doing something. It would be **prudent** to look both ways before crossing a busy street.

ragged: Something **ragged** is old, torn, or worn out. If your favorite book is three years old, you might notice it becoming **ragged**.

ranker: Something **rank** is growing very thickly. He walked carefully through the **rank** weeds. **Rank** also means that something has a strong or rotten smell. A swamp often smells **ranker** than a forest on dry land.

ransacked: If a place has been **ransacked**, it has been completely (and sometimes messily) searched, sometimes by someone looking for things to steal. I had to clean up my **ransacked** room once I found my missing library book. Tracks in our **ransacked** campsite showed that two bears had been there while we were hiking.

raspy: A **raspy** sound is harsh and scratchy. You might have a **raspy** voice when you have a cold.

recited: To **recite** something is to say or repeat it out loud. It is usually something you have learned by heart. We **recited** the Pledge of Allegiance every Friday at the school assembly. He was asked to **recite** a poem he had memorized.

reflected: When something is **reflected**, its image can be seen somewhere else, as though it's in a mirror. Sunlight is often **reflected** on drops of water. Also, to **reflect** about something is to think seriously and carefully about it. The class **reflected** on the meaning of the story they read.

rejoicing: An expression of joy. There was great **rejoicing** when we found out that school was cancelled because of a snowstorm.

repent: To **repent** is to feel deeply sorry for doing something. If you were to get angry and yell at your best friend, you might **repent** your actions later.

repercussions: A **repercussion** is an echo. You can hear the **repercussion** of your voice when you shout into a deep canyon. The drums made loud **repercussions** in the large, empty room.

reproachfully: If you act **reproachfully** toward someone, you blame that person for something or show that you are disappointed in that person. I looked **reproachfully** at my best friend when she admitted that she had lied to me. You might speak **reproachfully** to your dog for chewing up your new shoes.

resilient: Something or someone that is **resilient** is able to recover from difficult, rough, or painful actions. A thick plastic cup is **resilient** because it doesn't break if it falls to the floor. A **resilient** person might simply laugh and walk away from being teased.

resolved: When you **resolve** to do something, you make a firm decision to do it. He **resolved** to eat less sugar and more vegetables.

retorted: When you **retort**, you answer someone quickly and sharply. When the boy complained about his burnt toast, his brother **retorted** that he should make his own.

revived: To **revive** something is to give new strength or life to it. When I felt dizzy and sick on a hot day last summer, a glass of cool water **revived** me.

ridiculous: Very silly or foolish. She wore a **ridiculous** hat with plastic fruit and flowers all over it.

roomers: A **roomer** is someone who rents a room in another person's house or building. The woman down the street has a **roomer** who rents her guest bedroom.

roused: If you **rouse** someone, you wake her up. The smell of blueberry pancakes **roused** me out of bed this morning.

saber: A heavy sword with a long, curved blade.

savored: To **savor** something is to enjoy it greatly or fully. When you **savor** a meal, you taste each bite with great pleasure. I **savored** every minute of my summer vacation.

scoured: To **scour** is to clear out or clean with force. The ocean waves **scoured** shallow holes into the sand.

scrabbled: When you **scrabble**, you scrape or grab at something with your hands in a struggling way. The rabbit **scrabbled** to escape the thorny bush.

scrolls: A **scroll** is a roll of paper or parchment (specially prepared animal skin) with writing on it. The ends of **scrolls** are usually wrapped around a rod.

sheen: A shine on the surface of something. If you polish a piece of wooden furniture with oil, it will develop a nice **sheen**. Sweating puts a **sheen** on your skin.

sheerest: Something **sheer** is delicate and see-through. The girl's mother made her a scarf for the party out of the prettiest, **sheerest** fabric she could find.

slackening: Something that is **slackening** is becoming slower or less strong. A pilot starts **slackening** an airplane's speed when he comes in for a landing.

snarled: If you **snarl**, you speak in an angry or threatening way. I **snarled** "Go away or else!" at anyone who tried to bother me while I studied for my test.

snatch: To **snatch** something is to quickly take something that belongs to someone else. Someone **snatched** the bicycle from the yard. The police were looking for the person who **snatched** the money from the shop's counter.

solemn: Very serious. You might make a **solemn** promise never to lie to your best friend. He became **solemn** when he found out that his mother was in the hospital.

soughing: To **sough** is to make a sighing, moaning, or soft rustling sound. The children could hear something **soughing** and creaking as they crept through the abandoned house. **Sough** can rhyme with *cow* or *cuff*.

splendid: Something **splendid** is very beautiful or excellent. The male peacock displayed its **splendid** feathers to attract the nearby female. You might have a **splendid** meal if it's made with farm-fresh food.

square: If you **square** someone (or **square with** someone), you set things right with them. You might **square** your brother by apologizing for yelling at him. Or you might **square with** your friend by paying back the money she lent you last week.

stately: A **stately** person acts and looks noble and majestic. The queen held her head high and walked to her carriage in a **stately** manner. My father looks **stately** in his brand-new suit and tie.

sternly: Seriously and firmly. The captain **sternly** ordered his soldiers to march into battle.

stifling: If something is **stifling**, it causes you to have trouble breathing, usually because it is too hot or there isn't enough air. A room might be **stifling** if someone shuts all the windows and then turns the heat up very high.

stocky: A **stocky** person has a solid or heavy body. Weightlifters and professional football players often have a **stocky** build.

stricken: When you are **stricken**, you are in great pain, fright, or shock from something that has happened. You might be **stricken** if you saw a car accident or heard a strange scream in the middle of the night.

supped: When you **sup**, you eat supper. Last night we **supped** on fried chicken, potato salad, and corn on the cob.

surged: To **surge** is to rush forward with force. At the beach, a wave can **surge** forward suddenly and get you wet. The crowd **surged** forward to get a better view of the musician.

taunted: If you **taunt** someone, you mock or tease that person in a hurtful or scornful way. My older siblings **taunted** me because they have later bedtimes than I have. Someone might **taunt** you by offering you a piece of candy and then grabbing it away when you try to take it.

tempted: When you're **tempted** by something, you want it very much, even if it's wrong. If you were very hungry, you might be **tempted** to eat your lunch before lunchtime. He was **tempted** to open the gift he found in his mother's closet, even though his birthday was still a week away.

territory: A **territory** is an area of land, sometimes belonging to a certain person or group.

thatch: A **thatch** roof is made out of strong plant stalks, such as straw, reeds, or palm tree leaves.